555
Sticker Fun
Shopping

Licensed exclusively to Top That Publishing Ltd
Tide Mill Way, Woodbridge, Suffolk, IP12 1AP, UK
www.topthatpublishing.com
Copyright © 2014 Tide Mill Media
All rights reserved
4 6 8 9 7 5 3
Manufactured in Zhejiang, China

The best clothes shop

This clothes shop is the very best in town. Use the stickers to fill it with dresses, tops, bags, shoes and much, much more.

In the changing room

There is lots of space to try on clothes in the changing room.
Fill the cubicles with beautiful outfits.

Shoes, shoes and more shoes!

The girls cannot believe their luck. This shop has shoes for every occasion. Use the shoe stickers to make your own displays!

Perfume shop

The girls love this shop with its pretty bottles, beautiful boxes and amazing smells. Create perfume displays with the stickers.

Perfect accessories

Hats, gloves, sunglasses, bags! This shop sells all the accessories a girl could wish for. Use stickers to stock the display stands and keep the shoppers happy.

Gadgets galore

This shop sells the very latest technology. Use stickers to create fantastic gadget displays.

Fancy dress fun

This fancy dress shop sells awesome costumes and there are lots of giggling girls trying things on. Use stickers to complete the themed displays. It's such fun!

Café

The girls always stop at their favourite café. Fill the counter, tables and shelves with colourful crockery and delicious food.

Toyshop

It is time to buy some birthday presents and the toyshop is full of customers in search of the perfect gift. Stock the shop with toys of all kinds.

At the newsagent's

The girls are looking for magazines to enjoy when they get home.
Fill the newsagent's stand with a great selection.

Cake creations

This cake shop is famous for its amazing creations. Fill the counter with delicious delights for the girls to choose from. Add pretty cake boxes and bags for take-away treats.

Beautiful ballgowns

The school prom is in two weeks. Fill this fabulous dress shop with beautiful ballgowns and pretty accessories, so the girls have lots to choose from.

Fruit shop stop

It is time for something fresh and tasty to keep the tired shoppers going. Fill the fruit shop displays with healthy choices.

At the nail bar

There are lots of girls having manicures. Fill the nail bar with bottles of pretty polish and packs of false nails.

Supermarket dash

The girls' mums have asked them to go to the supermarket. Stock the shelves with groceries and special offers. Fill the trolley with things on their shopping list.

Hair and beauty

The girls love this beauty department full of glamorous luxuries.
Use the stickers to complete the displays. What will the girls try first?

The bookshop

It is quiet and cosy in the bookshop today with girls enjoying browsing and reading. Use the book stickers to fill the shelves and table displays.

In the sweet shop

Bags of sweeties are essential for the bus journey home! Fill the sweet shop shelves with jars of treats for the girls to choose from.

Buying sports kit

The girls need new sports kit for school. Luckily, this shop sells everything! Fill the displays with sports clothes and equipment.

Jewellery store

This jewellery store is expensive, but the girls have spotted some bargains. Complete the tempting displays by adding some beautiful necklaces and pretty trinkets.

Ice-cream parlour

It is time for ice cream! Fill the counter with lots to choose from and jars of decorations. Find a place for each girl to enjoy her cold, creamy treat.

Music shop

This shop has everything for music lovers. Stock its shelves with music to listen to, instruments to play and accessories for would-be pop stars.

A great gift shop

The girls are hunting for end-of-term gifts for their teachers.
Complete the displays with selections of gifts to suit all tastes.
Choosing should be easy!

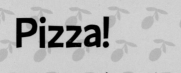

Pizza!

What makes the perfect end to the perfect shopping trip? Pizza, of course! Fill the kitchen with ingredients for the girls' pizza and food for the table.